The Ribbon Around the Bomb

poems by

Elizabeth Levine

Finishing Line Press
Georgetown, Kentucky

The Ribbon Around the Bomb

With gratitude for three of my dearest friends and muses,
who have passed away in recent years,
Carla Rodman, Dianne d'Etreillis Roussel and Regina Quattrochi.
It was Regina who gave me the book *Touched by Fire,*
by Kay Redfield Jamison, which inspired this collection of poems.
These three women stayed with me in the darkest of hours.
May their memory be for blessing.

Copyright © 2019 by Elizabeth Levine
ISBN 978-1-63534-829-3 First Edition
All rights reserved under International and Pan-American Copyright Conventions. No part of this book may be reproduced in any manner whatsoever without written permission from the publisher, except in the case of brief quotations embodied in critical articles and reviews.

Publisher: Leah Maines
Editor: Christen Kincaid
Cover Art: Dr. John Parras
Author Photo: Andy Cohen
Cover Design: Leah Huete

Printed in the USA on acid-free paper.
Order online: www.finishinglinepress.com
also available on amazon.com

Author inquiries and mail orders:
Finishing Line Press
P. O. Box 1626
Georgetown, Kentucky 40324
U. S. A.

Table of Contents

Introduction 1

The Ribbon Around the Bomb: Frieda Kahlo 3

The Homosexual Poet: Hart Crane 7

Strange Victory: Sara Teasdale 10

The Voyage Out: Virginia Woolf 13

Exile: Marina Tsvetayeva 14

The Bell Jar: Sylvia Plath 16

The Poetry of War: Randall Jarrell 19

The Garden of Earthly Delights: Frank O'Hara* 20

After Auschwitz: Paul Celan 22

Dream Songs: John Berryman 24

Confessions: Anne Sexton 26

The Last Man: Welden Kees 28

Introduction

I became interested in the subject of writers who committed suicide, particularly poets whose work I had studied and admired. Given the suicide of Kate Spade and Anthony Bourdain this past week, I would argue that creativity and mental illness are closely aligned; that the membrane is thin and that this connection bears further investigation. Nevertheless, as I began to read poetry again, my own desire to write returned. I hadn't written any poetry in eighteen years. Suddenly, I could not stop writing.

The poems that I have written are a fictionalized version of what I imagine these writers' final days or hours felt like. My interpretation is intuitive, not entirely factual, yet incorporates elements of their own biographies and poems in the telling of these final hours. I tried to imagine Frank O'Hara's last sunset on Fire Island. What Virginia Wolf might have thought as she chose the stones she deliberately placed in her pocket. I searched their work for clues, for words or images that repeatedly occurred. I searched for meaning.

Truth is imperfect and life even more so. The tipping point is different for each of us. Why is it that Sylvia Plath chose to kill herself on February 3, 1963? Why did Paul Celan commit suicide after being liberated from the camps? Is the reason why these artists committed suicide different for each individual, or is there a commonality in the final hours, regardless of circumstances? Is the decision to take ones' own life spurred by a particular incident? Or does cumulative exhaustion force them to make this choice? Is it surrender or is it relief or both?

I have included as my opening poem, "The Ribbon Around the Bomb," an homage to the life of Frida Kahlo, a Mexican painter whose work I admire. Unlike the other poems, Kahlo died of a pulmonary embolism at her beloved Blue House a week after her forty-seventh birthday. However, upon further investigation, there were rumors that she perhaps committed suicide. We will never know.

She died after an incredibly tumultuous marriage and divorce from Diego Rivera, a life of chronic pain, stemming from polio as a child and then her permanent injuries resulting from a bus accident when she was 18. Often, she would spend hours confined to bed or in corsets designed to correct her spinal injuries, yet somehow, she painted every day. When she finally had her first solo show, she arrived transported in her bed. Here is a woman who was unstoppable, and whose paintings now sell for $8 million dollars. Where did her fortitude and determination come from?

I wanted to contrast her life with the death of these writers. Why do some of us endure? Perseverance? I don't know. But I do know, where there is still life, there is still hope. May her story inspire us in the hours of doubt and despair, and may we discover the strength within ourselves to continue writing.

RIBBON AROUND THE BOMB: Frida Kahlo (1907-1954)

I.
I am thirsty and you are my thirst.
Diego,
I am wearing my purple panties
So you can take me
In the bathroom stall.
Here in Detroit,
Where entire city is painted grey.
Even your WPA murals
Can't carry color
To this city of cadavers
Skin is as white as cocaine,
as pallid as apathy.
Here we are
Forgotten fish
In a land of vapid words
Here in this foreign country
No man, like Neruda, names his house: *La Cascona*.
After the red drapes at the Y
Between his lover's legs.

II.
Take me home.
To our country,
The only land in the world
Naked of the letter A.
We come from elsewhere, from the land of lizards and tequila
This is where we reside:
In our marital bed of sketches pinned onto mosquito netting
With worn, wooden clothes pins,
Here we paint raw beauty in this unsanitary world.
I touch the moon inside you.
I taste your iron and your ore.
I see violet butterflies, little lilacs, licking.
I hear you swear: *¡Coño!*

I feel the safety of my wounded spine
Laying in the grey birch of your silver chest.

III.
You promise to love my lost leg
Your *promesa*
Echoes like a Neruda love sonnet.
Under the sweaty sheets,
We sing to each other of child barren
Injuries and polio: our sonnets of despair.
Cuídame, Diego
You build me a stepstool,
So I could climb up, up, up
And away onto our bed
Into the kingdom of faraway places.

IV.
The torrential tempest of our daily lives,
Our summer storm, this marriage and divorce,
Your affair with my sister
Her bare beautiful brazen brasos
Wrapped around the circumference of
Your thick, cheating neck.
Our arms are not white.
There is nothing white in our wild, wounded world.
In Mexico,
Our sky is perpetual turquoise, our ocean tourmaline,
Our forests emerald, our Blue House the color of rare sapphires.

V.
Aquí estoy Diego,
Aquí soy yo,
Mírame, véame
But no, already
You are sketching and smoking
Drawing, withdrawing.

I am coming Diego, I am coming.
Espérame. Wait for me.

VI.
Don't let the doctors
Bleach white coats and Satanic stethoscopes,
Like Black rat snakes
Wave prescription pads and surgical saws
Over my broken body. Don't let them amputate
My toes or threaten to sedate my untamed heart
that beats like bats wings in the darkness.

VII.
This is what I know:
I am made of breakable bones.
Yo soy quien soy.
Eres tú. Así es.
You wanted a silent student, an artist's model,
A woman the world wouldn't listen to.
But everyone hears my paintings screaming in Spanish.

VIII.
No one loses anything, Diego
We simply forget how
Important we once were to one another
How you are fumes I breathe,
Like a fire eater incinerating everything.

IX.
There's something wrong with me, Diego.
Algo me duele.
I need
to show you
My cellulite and amputation scars
I need
you to carry me across the
Forest of my dreams

So I can wave one last time to the Palm trees
Before the doctors lock me away.
I am so tired Diego!

X.
Love me like the red blood
of a bull, *Mi matador,*
Kill me out of respect, not spite.
Smash my porcelain heart.
Make of me a Mexican mural!
Exhibit my fragments, a grand mosaic,
In a museum
Goddess of the Sheaths,
The world will see what
We are made of
You and I
Show them!
In my wonderland there is no Alice
When I fall down the rabbit hole
A wilderness
Of braids: unborn daughters,
Mangled limbs,
A left foot's raw scar a razor's edge,
Memory itself a bloody machete through the heart.
All my red senses ablaze.
Why have we lost our paint?
What I remember is not what we lost
But what we found in one another.
Neruda's poemas
de amor y una
canción deseperada.

THE HOMOSEXUAL POET: HART CRANE (1899-1932)

I.
In Autumn,
I find love.
It makes me stand
Still on Second Avenue.
I find myself
At the crossroads
Of what I know and what I can't have.

I flee New York City for the Isle of Pines,
Escaping into self-imposed exile.
The landscape changes in the Southern Hemisphere
But I do not. Alas.
I devour Mexican men, yet they consume me.
My nights stripped down to the pelvis. Anonymous
and temporal as desire, violent in its urgency.
Beware the ides of my ravenous desire.

I carry transit papers stamped from fleeting encounters:
Forbidden. Their very names invisibly inked.
The sheer volume of them imprints my fragmented heart.
As if each encounter were an entry
A port, that has no name, deep
In the Devil's Triangle. A voyage,
An infinite journey, arriving nowhere
Circuitous in its route.
North or South, I destroy my bifurcated life.

II.
The drinking starts in Mexico but does not stop.
The cacti yearn for water beneath the San Salvador sun, their thirst,
Like mine, unslaked. It pricks the desert air. Insatiable.
My darkest days clenched into a mere
fist full of waking, coherent hours.
My tongue shrivels for want of whiskey. Parched.
The white Spanish styled haciendas blind me with convention,
Predictable clay tiled roofs trap secret disappointments within them
Red clay tiles entomb.
Rooftops, alter the proportion and structure of landscapes.

III.
Iguanas cry in the garden for Emil.
Their reptilian throats call his name each spring-weeping.
My drinking spikes after Emil leaves
It plummets and resurges,
Absent valleys for recovery.
I never return to land or to poetry.

I am left with
Seven types of ambiguity
Anger, Frustration, Doubt, Sex, Despair, Pride and Envy.
These I own now not poetry.

IV.
In Mexico I marry a woman.
Church bells weep in outrage
For my unabashed sin
Against God.
I chose Peggy only because
she belongs to someone else.
Because I can.
I steal heterosexual wishes:
Marriage, family, union.
Enough to satisfy the matrix of her unknowing heart.
But not my heart. Not this homosexual heart.

V.
I return to New York City, Divorce:
having failed myself and others.
A Lexington Avenue subway train speeds along tracks
Absent a conductor.
The subway speaks my language: screeching brakes, piercing noise
Sheer volume more than sound.
Stations announce themselves, as if
I had a destination rather than mere memory.
The sky scrapers twinkle like stars, whispering Mount Us!

VI.
Poetry tortures me now.
Men, reduced to
ambiguous pronouns packaged in back rooms
With small spaces and stale air,
Caught at the intersection
Of straight and narrow,
Abstinence and ambivalence.
I arrive at the month of April
Unable to explain how March has disappeared.
Florida calls me like a siren. Self-propulsion.
Bereft of a captain to steer the adagios of islands
Past the danger of shipwreck.
I adopt the personality of a sailor, fleeing Columbus, fleeing anything
Remotely Spanish. Like the Inquisition.
Catholicism.

VII.
I cast a fisherman's net.
Love swims past me,
A shadow in the water, fins and tail.
I grasp at life jackets, neon-orange,
Dream of rescue
By a search party sent to save me
From the slavery of self.
I board the battleship, climb the mast above everyone's
Predictions.
The Ocean awaits me, it's callous eye wide and welcoming,
whispering my name. *Yes, I am Hart Crane.*
What is left of what I know and can bear without hatred remains
poetry.

STRANGE VICTORY: SARA TEASDALE (1884-1933)

I.
Love songs
Cannot impede the flame and shadow
Of my darkest moon.
The mirror of my heart bears
A sinister jagged edge,
Renders musical chords to shards
Dismember
Melody my sorrowful notes.
Reverence and joy vanished,
Symphonies long forgotten
Limp lullabies
Sung by grieving mothers
To their stillborn children.
Harmonies of restraint and regret,
Echoes of Missouri mornings
Spent flattened by the solitude of a
Sick childhood. Confinement.
A decade of illness
Behind a closed door
Hidden in a second story suite
Of loneliness and imposed privacy.

II
When I was ten I turned
The wide-open world on its axis.
Its outstretched hands beckoned me:
School.
Then the women who spun the Potters' Wheel
Help shape my song.
Then stifled words ran, unshielded
Rivers to the sea
Their perpetual leaving an infinite stanza.

III
I marry and move
Far from the flat, vapid plains

To New York City
Where neighbors
On Central Park
Cannot withstand
The stock market crash.
From my window I see
Men in pin striped suits jumping,
Bodies falling from buildings.
The edges of the atlas
Akin to my own suicidal thoughts,
Slip under the apartment door,
Uninvited guests.

IV
I wish
My marriage to a good man
Who loves the music of my poetry,
Were a fleece comforter,
Soft, seductive silk sheets
To assuage my frail bones.
But it is Helen of Troy,
Vachel my lover
Who visit me in my lugubrious dreams.
Perfect lyrical poetry,
A symphony of beautiful syllables, even
The Pulitzer prize,
Console me less
Than divorce.

IV.
The epoch for love. Ephemeral.
Vachel long married with children
Then these two brutal years buried
In the unforgiving earth. Suicide. A poet's death.
The lateral wings of my broken-hearted hands
Weep for his departure.

My poetry changes to perpetual rain,
Mourning,
Losing their lyricism.

V.
I shall not care
About April or the leaves
Of cherry blossoms, peony pink.
Every flower abandons
Its garden, bitter thorns and drought
Break upon their blooms.

VI.
As if in a dream sleeping pills
Slide down the cavernous void of my aching
Thirst: *Vachel*. An insatiable thirst
That neither fame nor poetry can slake.

THE VOYAGE OUT: VIRGINIA WOOLF (1882-1941)

From my room I see the befogged lighthouse,
Joyless, the British morning apologizes.
This greyness enters my bones
Reducing my exterior life to fog.
Suddenly my surroundings appear foreign
as if I have traveled abroad
without leaving my own room.
My days rendered so monotonous
That even a change in season anticipates nothing.
Perpetually gloomy, devoid of light.
I avoid dangerous emotions;
they are too expensive, exhausting.
Perhaps it was wartime when I forfeited optimism
Every day, the English stoicism
subtly settles in my walk, my gestures
Indeed, I abandon the trappings of my own routine.
I have journeyed beyond pragmatism, arriving
At resignation.

I sit at my desk.
Finish the letter to my husband.
The last letter. I seal it and place it on my desk, next to my journal
Absent an entry for today. Writing eludes me, nor
Do I struggle to find words, rather find solace in the blank page?

I approach the stream eager, the urgent need
To find five perfect black stones,
weight enough for each pocket.
I slip the stones into my blazer.
On its way to the river, the water falls over boulders, one, the heaviest
The tongue of my regrets.

EXILE: MARINA TSVETAYEVA (1892-1941)

All that remains of Czechoslovakia are my poems.
My prison poems bear witness to the constellation of bodies.
Fallen in the resistance, a jarring narrative.
How she survives the German invasion, only the dead can answer.

They took the mountains and the sea and the sun from us,
Until there was nothing left to plunder or steal.
My former country defies translation, a storm of collaborators.
Her complicity blackens the hands of the survivors.

My son and I are exiled to Russia,
eating wilted cabbages and disgrace,
Surviving merely on memories,
Stanzas of revenge and return.
The borders of grief follow us and corrode my poetry.
We arrive in Moscow carrying only suitcases of rage.

In Russia, the government assassinates my husband.
Now I am no longer any man's wife or mistress

My daughter's slow death, not as merciful as a bullet.
She starves in prison, hungry for family or mercy.
There is no translation
For the Czech word *freedom* in Siberia.
Russians need not romantic words, just boots
To march across winter,
The train stations were so dreary
I would not even stop at them,
If I still had choices.

Now, my son and I live so far east of any witnesses
we grow forgotten. Obscurity
has no words, no vowels, no punctuation: Infinite.
Our village of shame appears on no map.
The punishment of being forgotten flattens me.

We relieve ourselves in the cold wind against
Which my private orifices freeze shut,
Like barnyard animals, livestock
We resemble animal husbandry.
When storms press,
We gather outside absent
the nobility of an umbrella,
Catch rain in empty bins and bottles,
or lonely ration cans if rations run out. Rations always run out.
The taste of tin like rusted nails on the tongue
Leaves an acrid residue.
I dream of factories spouting water from their crematorium chimneys.
I dream of ovens. Famine has a taste.

THE BELL JAR: SYLVIA PLATH (1932-1963)

I.
January enters the house and finds me absent of resolutions.
The coldest winter in English history invades my bones.
Snow and isolation blankets the roofs of Devon's cottages,
Covers my frigid neighbors' loneliness and regrets.
This weary white landscape, sterile with frost
Reminds me of British manners.
Icicles form on barren trees in my husband's heart
waiting to impale me.
My illness seeps into the walls, the crevices of windows,
Slides silently under the door jam, permeating the whole house.
I forget to bathe or take out the rubbish,
Women's work, tasks Ted expects from me.

II.
My children Nicholas and Frieda grow
Hungry and ill.
Grimy from my negligence,
Their frightened faces haunt me. As if they
Were cherubic ghosts, wandering the hallways,
Screaming out to me at night from the land of nightmares.
I understand nightmares.
I warn Ted
"Take the children.
Go to your mothers. I need to write."
I must return to the warmth of words.

III.
The month endures but I cannot.
By February, I am withering before the cold.
It is a new semester, a new affair, every term
My husband fucks another co-ed.
I learn how to pretend.
I pretend not to know.
When I call him in London, she answers the telephone.
She is our new tenant. I imagine
Her long, pale, traitor's legs, splayed out on our marital bed

We shared. A history ago.
Her voice tells me she does not yet know
His cheating bones, his liar's heart.
She visited us once this past summer.
I fed her from my own vegetable garden, honey and edible flowers,
Fresh cut sage.
I served her dinner on my mother's emerald ringed china:
A wedding gift.
Betrayal hardens me, makes me dangerous,
Provokes me to do unimaginable things.

IV.
I read the works of Anne Sexton, Sara Teasdale, Virginia Wolff.
Winter is the suicidal season for women who write.
I recall vaguely the upwards of 400 poems I wrote at Smith College
In a dormitory painted buttercup yellow,
and can't remember one complete line. Even
titles elude me.

The hours drag the day along with a lurch. Only Ariel inspires me now.
I light the fire in the hearth, watch the blue- orange flames
sputter and fail. Chemistry.
Dawn comes and fades somehow into dusk.
The next morning is flat and grey, like the one before it.
I sit in the kitchen in my flannel bathrobe,
where I nurse my tea and my despair.
I smoke a cigarette and watch the birds migrate south,
Searching for warmth.
I suddenly think of my German father in our kitchen in New England,
Drinking his tumbler of bourbon, his rage bubbling up beneath
The surface of things. The wait for violence.
And bug collection, displayed under a glass dome
Bulging like an evil eye, watching.

V.
I should eat and take my medication.
Yet, I turn on the oven to prepare a meal.
I find no utility in these quotidian gestures without

Ted to watch me fail.
I place towels under the doorway to my children's bedroom.
I take comfort in knowing that I have fallen so far, I can fall no further.

THE POETRY OF WAR: RANDALL JARRELL (1914–1965)

They say I am a war poet but I find no poetry in war,
No beautiful words for who I have become.
What I have witnessed troubles me even if I shut my eyes.
To simple truths.
The art of war is leaning what to overlook and what stays with me;
I survive the war, own a purple heat to cover what lays underneath,
Permanently broken.
But I feel just as dead as those bodies left behind,
Buried in a country of temples and whores,
where no earth or holy water rendered
Death dignified.

I still remember the blood of strangers,
the smell of a village burning, no men remained.
The war has eaten them, giving birth to a countryside
Of widows and orphans who know life
Is suffering. Everywhere, I see strewn limbs of soldiers
I had breakfast with earlier that morning.
Random hands I once played poker with,
Our cigarettes the only light in a starless, Godless night
Flattened by the heat, by the stench, by the obligation.
Somewhere in the merciless night babies cry.
Dogs are slaughtered for food.
When I return home after the war,
I hear perpetual barking.
I am fifty-one. Half of my life has been spent killing others.
The other half is too frightening to contemplate.
It is 1965 when I leave the Veteran's Hospital and begin the walk home.
I think of the volume of loss and the shape it takes at dusk.

THE GARDEN OF EARTHLY DELIGHTS: FRANK O'HARA (1926-1966)

The Pines beckon me: the garden of earthly delights.
Men who smell of tangerines,
Men who taste of salt and sand,
Men whose names I leave behind in the dunes.
Few share breakfast.
Fewer still survive the summer; they fade into fall
Pass like dreams; do not assume
Space or permanence.

I am not lonely or burdened with regrets.
I clean the ashtrays, dust the walls and wash the sheets.
I refuse to be anyone else, or suffer intricate days.
I mix Mimosas and turn on the record player.
Peggy Lee sings, *"Is that all there is?"*
I answer gleefully, *"Yes Peggy! That is all there is."*

Fingers in sunlight, cocktails at dusk, sunsets, ocean,
stars that burn brighter fueled by our hedonistic mistakes:
Only these are permanent.

September ends and my friends and I leave Fire Island
Like migrant farm workers
In search of strawberries and scorching California heat.
My friends feed me stories
During the endless melancholy of autumn.
Shelter me through the cruel eternal winter,
We dream only of men, night, ice in the blue glass.
We don't lie to each other, only ourselves.
I am undone by the generosity
Friends display with their faith in me.
I know myself, however.
I will never be mentally sober.
For, like summertime, I lack integrity.
In fact, when summer spreads open its
Sand dunes and High Tea,
I stumble and fall into a vortex.

Another season of infinite strangers and exquisite gestures,
The soft, unblemished flesh above the inside of the right wrist,
A Bombay martini on a man's breath,
Olives I suck out of his mouth, swallow.
One night, lust betrays me, what I know
As certain fails me. Suddenly,
Dunes turn sinister, absent stars.
The safety of my own home disappears
Too far, too dark, too distant.

I flag down a beach taxi, too drunk to journey home.
I lie down in the dunes after tea, waiting,
My pocket of pocket of rhinestones instead of Orion,
For the strength to find the next man. Mystery,
My body forms a starfish in the sand.
My lonely unabashed bones
Seduce like the open flesh of the world.
There is nothing left with which to venture forth
except the lassitude of delirium.
I am rendered a dead man's voice, reciting the echo
Beautiful lies spoken in every conceivable language.

*The Garden of Earthly Delights is the title of a painting by Hieronymous Bosch

AFTER AUSCHWITZ: PAUL CELAN (1920-1970)

Auschwitz makes me illegitimate.
The Germans orphan me,
Bastardize my gypsy blood,
Erasing Romania.
Until there is no nationality left for me except
To wander the geography of despair.
The camps execute my mother,
Strike my father with typhoid,
I assume the guilt of survival,
Laboring under its Sisyphus weight.

In prison, I dreamed of women
in black stockings, red lipstick
Cigarettes.
But the days of pleasure long past.
Oceans of Jews fall like flames,
Rendering them ash.
Undignified, the dead walk beside me.
They lie down in graves like dry leaves.
They leave imprints. their bony fingers outstretched,
Reaching for God.
I engrave what is left in my memory,
But never speak of it.
I remember only digging, covered shovels,
Mud and the infinite grey of internment
Treeless and silent, void of clouds, the color of distance.
I bury my faith in their graves; No
Coffin can accommodate this many dead.
The trains and whistles are what I carry in me now.
The harsh sound of German words invades my speech
Like the noise of marching boots and apprehension.
Brutality is explicit, guttural.
Who prays and who weeps I cannot be sure.
All of us are orphans after liberation.
It is a diaspora of survivors.
Slowly, deliberately, some
Friends die in different countries killed

By suicide.
They disintegrate. Shatter from what we have seen.
In Paris, I dream of the blue-eyed guards
in a place that can't be named.
Only the choking lessons of chimneys remain:
My permanent aversion to fire.
My complete refusal to say Kaddish,
Gagging on Aramaic words, the taste of hardship,
A bile I swallow. Barbaric, how the Germans
Contaminate our rituals of grief, rendering us
Mute. I can't remember anymore what things were called before the war.
Liberated by Americans, I am nevertheless permanently a Jew.
My blue-inked arm, tattooed with my prison number reminds
Me of who I am, lest I forget.
I choose the Seine
Because baptized by the beauty of the river
In the City of Lights
After years of darkness and the death of stars,
I want to be washed clean of guilt. Even if I could forget
Where I have come from, whom I lost, what I have become,
Even Paris cannot wash off the indelible scar.

DREAM SONGS: JOHN BERRYMAN (1914-1972)

I
I rub cold hands
Spit sour breath
To ward off chill.
November in Minnesota
Tastes like despair;
It is that cold.

I will always hate winter.
It means dying, freezing, dying.
Death tastes of frost,
Of blue lips kissing stilllborn children,
Leaves small scars
Like a crucifix.

II
I wake up wet with sweat,
Press my face with red, raw wrists
Cannot remember.
What did happen in St. Paul?
I must write.
Poems clog my pores, strangle me
On the Pulitzer Prize
The umbilical cord that fucks us both.

III
6:27 a.m.
I drive by rows, screaming rows of working class
Homes with their common dreams and ordinary defeats.
Henry hates anything ordinary.
Fog smudged, these vulgar edifices scream out
In protest, tobacco tarnished tombstones
Belching smoke into the night.
Brutal how my students, my lovers, my family's
Urgent voices assault my senses,
Like the screeching noises made by
rats who fly through trees,

Masquerading as birds.
Liars, whores, Sycophants
I will not miss them.
Instead, I follow in my father's footsteps,
Absent Florida or firearms.
I find my own way back home, to him.

IV
The slate, stale sky
The silver steel of the bridge spread below me
Like an eager virgin,
Old with open arms and legs.
Life is rich with dirt and joy
While I grovel amidst unfinished poems,
dream with open eyes of Redemption,
then shrug shoulders, swear, stub out my cigarette,
flick it from the ledge, watch it fall like tears.
On the bridge, layered with a scum of ice,
I tear pieces of poems like divorce proceedings
Then throw them up to greedily swallow air.
I watch them float, like failure,
Dusting the ice.
I cross my legs and want for nothing.

CONFESSIONS: ANN SEXTON (1928-1974)

I.
I am a woman poet,
I do not write about birds or nature.
Unimportant, compared to human experience:
A man's hands, the passage of time, the change from light to darkness.
 I write about the things I know:
Regrets, resolutions, relationships, remorse.
I write about the secret of being foreign, my excesses, and my darkness
This addled existence, the intimacy of dreams and ghosts.
The defeat of loving, being loved or not loved,
Hurting and being hurt,
Misery and happiness, children and spouses.
My bitter true poems fail to be sweet or pretty or maternal.

II.
My journey towards madness accelerated with loneliness
Inherited from previous generations. The aching absence of my daughters.
Out of habit, I sleep with men.
Flattened by
The universal way how, as a woman,
I fade from neglect, or shame, or grow old or forgotten.
Each pregnancy makes me more ill, more exhausted by responsibilities.
Motherhood feels to me like incarceration, like happy hour
Without cocktails, Sobering.
Unsteady with the burden of my daughters,
I relinquish custody of them. Another failure.
Far better to be treated for my crimes, executed in open air,
Guilty of keeping company with my own dangerous instincts.
Then suffer under the relentless demands motherhood asks of me,

Its unbearable drudgery far more debilitating than my
Previous mistakes, Sacrifice
Even worse than despair.
I forfeit my children, my husband, my family obligations.

III.
I lose months, then entire seasons, some more brutal than others.
The shape of my days become random and distorted.
Winter happens. Another year is gone.
Adrift, I drown in depression, grow desperate.
I miss Sylvia.
By June, I grow weary of being brave.

The smell of alcohol and valium permeate my skin, like perfume.

IV.
I must return to the familiarity of the Westwood Lodge.
On my own volition, I commit myself to the hospital.
The bars on the windows steal the air.
I fuck my doctor because it is an old behavior, like adaptation.
In the cell next to me, a man rants about his mother and her betrayal.
I understand betrayal.
When my parents die, I am left with only my mothers' fur coat
And my fathers' brutality as my inheritance.
Words take shape, but I put the poems away.
For now, I row across the lake searching for God
I visit the cemetery and wonder what the dead know,
And what the living keep secret.

THE LAST MAN: WELDON KEES (1955)

I.
Before
I vanish
I call the wrong friend.
Another mistake.
But I ask the right question.
"What keeps you going?"
She is too distracted by her own tragedies
And oppressive obligations
To formulate an answer worth staying for.
I cannot bear to be
Anyone's obligation
Other than my own.

II.
The distance between two points
is not a line but a circumference,
Leading me back to a
Lonesome cylinder,
The volume of which is perpetually empty.
The faraway suddenly nearby,
Just beyond reach.
I long for Hart Crane's Mexico,
The man, the poet:
I admire his noble and nefarious ways.

III.
What remains?
A 1954 Plymouth Savoy
Abandoned at the skirt
Of the Golden Gate Bridge,
A pair of red socks
Bleeding in a sink,
My cat howling for its master.
What is missing?
My wallet, my watch, my sleeping bag,

My savings account bank book:
Eight hundred dollars left of a long, lonesome life.

IV.
I leave no evidence
That I straddled this county,
One leg resolutely planted on each coast,
Dreaming of water,
A city to call home,
Fleeing Nebraska hardware stores,
False starts, the state of Colorado,
Denver and its unleashed potential.
Only San Francisco
Allows me to become absent from my own life.
A cigarette, a trim mustache, a dagger my outline
Of the life of a mind.

V.
If Renaissance men were defined
By their failure rather than their accomplishments,
I would be Galileo, Einstein,
The theory of relativity.
The man who discovered the world is
Flat, not round, as we imagined it to be.

VI.
Who will take custody
Of my wife Ann?
Whom I committed to the asylum,
Her paranoia and her Swans
Her feral fear of the McCarthy trials
Driving her to drink.

VII.
How they try to revive my reputation,
Unearth my poetry,
Which I have long ago abandoned,

Flickering with possibilities,
Now no more than a brief habitual
Glance in a rearview mirror
As I journey to unknown
Destinations: countries, metropolises, bodies of water.
Absent papers or passport,
I enter as an intruder,
Sliding instead my short stories,
The secret password. across the border
Let me in!

VIII.
I am the ancient Japanese tradition
Of ghost stories and an orange moon.
I am an unmade bed,
A photographic dark room,
A Cubist collage,
A Provincetown dune lost to the hurricanes.

IX.
The porchlight comes on in early November,
Reminding me of leaves I once raked
But never knew well.
Like I no longer know my own poems,
Or films, or friends or jazz.
What I know now is
Saturday rain,
A Slow Parade
Copies that never existed
Printed in black and white,
Unpublished in my poet's pockets.
I'm no longer doing what I want to do: Poetry
But is Anyone?

X.
The Last Man
Is the engraving I choose
For my tombstone
After thirty-nine poems
Disappear with me
Into the scaffolding of ordinary days.
An influence
On future generations
I will not live long enough to witness.

XI.
I don't bother to unpack.
I am not staying long.
Please say nothing of the obvious.
Things don't go well
Or as planned.
What a lovely party failure
Has been, a festivity that takes too long to
Arrive and for which I was
Psychologically unfit to attend.
I am the Great Depression
And the Rocky Mountain Review.
I am an acute triangle.
I am the Fall of Magicians:
My disappearance the ultimate
Slight of hand.

Acknowledgments

I would be remiss if I did not thank certain individuals for their guidance and support in compiling this chapbook over five long and difficult years. First, I would like to thank Finishing Line Press, my publisher, for their ongoing support of emerging writers and for the niche they occupy in representing writers who are struggling with grief and bereavement. I credit Leah Maines, Publisher, M.Div, for her assistance in facilitating this process, having aided many a wounded poet along his or her journey.

Then there are my two sons Jake and Alex Samieske who forgave me for the many hours spent writing when I did not attend their soccer games. I thank my parents, particularly my mother Ronnie Levine, who read multiple drafts.

I would also like to thank the M.F.A. Faculty at William Paterson University's English Department, particularly my Thesis Advisor Professor Martha Witt and Dr. John Parras, former Coordinator of the M.F.A. Program and Editor of the WPU online literary journal, MAP Literary.www.mapliterary.org, where I served as an intern. For poets who read this manuscript, I urge you to submit your poetry to this wonderful electronic publication.

I have had the privilege of studying at the Poetry Center at Passaic Community College for the past five years. www.poccpoetrycenter.edu. Under the direction and guidance of Maria Gillian, Executive Director of the Poetry Center at POCC and Laura Boss, Editor of Lips, I have attended poetry workshops which resulted in the first, and my favorite poem, "Ribbon Around the Bomb". "Witness: A Homage to Randall Jarrell", now entitled "The Poetry of War" was selected by the Hudson Valley Writer's Center for inclusion in its Seventh Annual War and Poets Event in 2012.

Lastly, I would like to thank fellow writers and poets who have encouraged me. A big shout out to Captain David Blacklock, who appears every twenty-five years to bring me back to shore when I have gone adrift. Other friends and colleagues include Clemencia

Molina, Julie Hansen, my Aunt Martha Reingold, author, poet and advocate, Val Oliver, my friend and copy editor, and Frank a.k.a. "Diego" Nicoletti, my editor and biggest fan. I would also like to thank the Montclair Write Group and Carl Sellinger, my favorite facilitator. Ironically, I would like to thank literary agent Sydelle Kramer, who advised me to "lose the poetry. You will never make a living as a poet." Not only was she right, her advice prompted me to write my novel, *What Remains,* which is currently being adapted as a play under the title "And She Was There." And she was.

Elizabeth Levine earned her M.F.A. in Creative Writing from the William Paterson University, where she works as Adjunct Faculty in the English Department and served as an intern for the English Department's online literary journal Map Literary. Her bilingual poem "La Lotería" and "After the Drive By" and "Scavenger Girl" have been published in the Montclair Write Group Sampler. Her second poetry chapbook, *God Doesn't Live at Our House Anymore.* is a collection of poems that directly relates to her identity as a mother before and after her daughter's death. Her third chapbook, *Ranting,* deals with social justice issues including immigration, higher education, and criminal justice. Her fourth chapbook *Savage* is a collection of poems about addiction and mental illness.

Her novel, *What Remains*, written under the pseudonym Charlotte Clear, is currently being adapted as a play under the title "And She Was There." Levine's novel deals with themes of trauma and resiliency. One of the chapters, "Powerless," which takes place in Bolivia and is written in English and Spanish, was chosen and produced as a Selected Short by the New Jersey Playwrights in the first New Jersey Selected Shorts in 2015. A second chapter, "What Is Lost" was selected for the Creative Writing Panel of the North Eastern Modern Language Association's International Conference in Toronto, Canada. Chapter 3, "Gay Geography," will be published by *MAPLITERARY*, the William Paterson English Department's online literary journal.

Ms. Levine writes trilingual poetry, non-fiction, fiction and creative non-fiction.

www.ingramcontent.com/pod-product-compliance
Lightning Source LLC
LaVergne TN
LVHW041504070426
835507LV00012B/1311